Praise for the Budgetnista

 Melissa ~~Name~~ Thanks again Tiffany TheBudgetnista! You SAVED my life literally! to some it's may be just money but everything was at stake for me. God bless you!!!

 The Whole Woman Project shared your photo.
The Budgetnista is not just telling you how to get out of debt but she keeps it real about her getting out of debt. Love The Budgetnista.

 Allison ~~Name~~ ▸ **Tiffany TheBudgetnista**
1 hr · 🌐

Thanks Tiffany TheBudgetnista you make budgeting and saving so much fun. 😊

 Lauren ~~Name~~ Lol! Tiffany TheBudgetnista, you really have no clue how many times a day your name, or the name of your group is mentioned in this household! You have truly changed the way the hubby and I look at money and credit! I thank you and I hope that people don't scroll past this post but instead actually get involved and get right! 😊

 Maya ~~Name~~ @Educ8Money2Kids   12m
Love how @TheBudgetnista defines money. Money is a tool. It can be used to build or destroy your financial life. YOU determine how it's used

 Rachel ~~Name~~ @TheBelleAgency   27 Dec
Was able to lower my car insurance today after going deeper into @TheBudgetnista's book. Y'all are sleeping if you haven't gotten it yet.

Praise for the Budgetnista

 Lorraine 23 hours ago LINKED COMMENT
Oh my gosh! I think you are wonderful!! Come Jan 1 I'm planning on paying down my debt!! You came along at a PERFECT time! Your plan makes so much sense! Your book is on its way!! You are a God send!! I'll keep in touch to let you know how it's going. While waiting for the book I'll be watching your YouTube videos! I'm so excited!!! Thank you for sharing your knowledge! ~Lorraine

 Radiant Yes ! Yes! Tiffany TheBudgetnista is defying all types of gender bias, stereotypes, and shattering glass ceilings in the financial advising profession! She getting all bicostal, cross-gender, and multi-socioeconomic..Go head Tiff!!!

Side note: I sincerely appreciate this awe-inspiring group of individuals. (((((Virtual Hugs))))

 Elizabeth
Today I took the first step in living the way I would like instead of waiting for the lottery to bless me I was able to make a sizeable donation to a friend's business, and I couldn't stop talking about how you helped make it possible, Tiffany TheBudgetnista Aliche! One of my goals this year is to support projects that help us grow as a community. Some people think I have a lot of money, but a little bit at a time adds up to something great!

Like · Comment · Stop Notifications · 3 hours ago via mobile

 Latrice Tiffany TheBudgetnista, I just finished listening to your podcast interview and it is inspiring to know that someone just like everyone else has experienced financial hardships that are relatable to ours and is not judgemental; but enjoy sharing your wealth of information to help the rest of us to live or best lives. Thanks!

Praise for the Live Richer Challenge

 Khalilah _____ Keep me posted Tiffany TheBudgetnista if they want someone on the East Coast! The whole challenge was a huge blessing for me! The biggest benefit I received from the challenge is a new mindset. My thinking has totally been transformed as a result of the LRC. That is priceless and something that can never be taken away from me!!! #Blessed and thanks again Tiffany for the passionate work that you do!

1 min · Unlike · 👍 1

 Chiniqua _____ ▸ **Dream Catchers : LIVE RICHER**
16 hrs · 🔼

I've been in this group for a while and never posted anything. Just wanted to share a little today. Before I started the challenge I had a maxed out credit card, all of my bills were past due, I had multiple pay day loans, and a credit score in the 400s. I had a shopping problem and continued to shop and waste money knowing my bills weren't paid. Sometimes I had to borrow money from my mother to get to work. It took an eviction notice and my cable getting cut off for me to wake up.

I found the challenge and it really helped me to get my priorities straight. It took a lot of hard work. I had to cut everything that was not necessary out of my budget. No shopping trips. No spending $15 a day eating out. No buying expensive gifts. I learned to do my own hair and nails. I bring my lunch everyday. I learned how to coupon and actually enjoy being cheap.

I'm finally caught up on all my bills, credit card is paid off, and I even opened my first savings account. It feels so good knowing I don't owe money to anyone and have a little nest egg. Thanks Tiffany for creating the challenge and everyone in the group for all the great advice you post. 😊

Dedicated to my Dream Catchers. It's more than money, we're a movement.

– Live Richer

Tiffany "The Budgetnista" Aliche

Let's get to know each other.

Hi, I'm Tiffany. Welcome to the beginning of your savings journey! If you're ready to stash more cash and to live a more abundant life, you've come to the right place.

To LIVE RICHER means to purposefully and passionately design the life you deserve. The purpose of the *LIVE RICHER Challenge: Savings Edition* is to teach you how to grow your savings and make more so you can lead the life you desire.

Although I received a financial education growing up, I haven't always made the best money choices. I love to share my story because it proves that no matter how bad a situation may seem, it's possible to dig your way out.

Tiffany's Financial Fiascos

1. At age 24, I took a $20,000 cash advance from my credit card and invested it with a "friend". This genius move landed me in $35,000 worth of debt a few months later.

2. At age 26, I bought my first home—right before the housing bubble burst. The value of my $220,000 condo declined to $150,000 in less than a year.

3. At age 30, as a result of losing my job during the Recession and being unable to keep up with my bills, the 802 credit score I once enjoyed quickly plummeted to 574.

Pretty bad, huh? Once I adopted my LIVE RICHER lifestyle, I was able to pay off my credit card debt in two and a half years, make peace with my mortgage lender, and raise my credit score almost 200 points in two years. I've even been able to travel to over 20 countries within the last few years.

Now, I use the solutions that helped me during my Financial Fiascos as a tool to guide people like you, who want to do the same.

In 2008, I started The Budgetnista, an award-winning professional and educational services firm. As "The Budgetnista", I'm a spokesperson—I also speak, write, teach and create financial education products and services that include seminars, workshops, curricula, and trainings.

I've written a bestselling book, *The One Week Budget* (a #1 Amazon best-seller), which teaches readers how to budget their income and automate the process over a period of just seven days. In 2015, I launched the first edition of the LIVE RICHER Challenge (you are currently reading the 2nd book in this series), which helped over 20,000 women across the world save over $4 Million and pay off over $500,000 worth of debt. I also wrote another #1 Amazon Bestseller called the *LIVE RICHER Challenge.* The book you're reading now is the second in my LIVE RICHER series.

You can learn more about me and The Budgetnista at www.thebudgetnista.com.

Why do this challenge?

Enough about me. Let's talk about you. Have you ever asked yourself any of these questions?

1. How do I make a budget?
2. How can I save money if I'm living paycheck to paycheck?
3. What can I do to pay for things I desire in life?
4. How can I make more money outside of my 9-to-5?

If so, great! This challenge will answer all of these questions, plus more! I even promise to do so in a straightforward way that'll be easy for you to implement. In just 22 days, you'll have a plan to accomplish your savings goals.

HOW TO READ THIS BOOK

Are you ready to start saving like a pro? Good, let's get to work.

How it works:
Each day I'll assign an Easy Financial Task designed to help you get and stay on the road to saving more money.

The daily tasks will focus on the money theme of the week. The weekly themes for the LIVE RICHER Challenge: Savings Edition are:

Week 1: Savings Mindset
Week 2: Implementation & Automation
Week 3: Increase Your Abundance
Final Day: LIVE RICHER

How to guarantee your success:
  • Every morning, read and commit to the Easy Financial Task.

  • Perform the task. Don't worry; it won't be hard.

  • Get an accountability partner(s). The best way to rock this Challenge is to partner up with at least one other person and work together. It'll keep you motivated. You can also reach out to and work with other Dream Catchers (the name I've given to folks working on the Challenge), in the private LIVE RICHER **forum** at www.livericherchallenge.com

  • Share your experiences with me, ask questions, and leave comments via social media. You can find me online here:

The Budgetnista Blog: thebudgetnistablog.com
Twitter & Instagram: @TheBudgetnista
Facebook: The Budgetnista

I have created many awesome resources for you that can't fit into this book. You can also find them for free at www.livericherchallenge.com.

LIVE RICHER,
Tiffany "The Budgetnista" Aliche

Table of Contents

Table of Contents

WEEK 1: SAVINGS MINDSET

THIS WEEK'S GOAL:

To overhaul the way you think about saving by changing your Saving Mindset.

Live Richer Challenge: Savings Edition
Day 1: Savings Goals

Week 1: Savings Mindset

Today's Easy Financial Task: Choose your savings goals, write them down, and share them with someone.

How to rock this task:
- List up to three specific savings goals.
- Post them in a place you'll see daily like on the fridge.
- Share your goals with me or a friend.

Welcome to your first day of the LIVE RICHER T: Savings Edition!
This week we're tackling your Saving Mindset. It doesn't matter how much money you make; if you don't have the right tools, attitude, or knowledge about saving, you won't be able to stack your coins.

For the first day of this Challenge, I want you to identify your specific savings goals. For example, "I want to save $600 in six months". Write your goals down and place them somewhere where you will see them every day to keep them in the forefront of your mind. Then share them with someone you trust.

For your goals to be most effective, make sure they answer these three questions:
1) What? ("I will save $600.")
2) When? ("I will save $600 by October 16th.")
3) How? (I will save $600 by October 16th by reducing my phone bill and packing my lunch for work each day.")

Now all that's left to do is to choose an accountability partner or partners. I highly recommend that you choose a partner or organize a group of people who are also participating in the Challenge so you can work together through the tasks.

If you can't find anyone, reach out to other Dream Catchers (the name I've given folks that are working on the Challenge). You can find us at www.livericherchallenge.com, once there click the tab marked "forum". There are thousands of Dream Catchers who would love to be your accountability partner!

Why is this task so important?
1) Putting your goals on paper gives them power.
2) Keeping them somewhere visible serves as a constant reminder.
3) Sharing them with others will hold you accountable.

So, let's get to it! Write down your goals. I've created a goal sheet for you. You can find this free resource at www.livericherchallenge.com under the book resources tab (Day 1: Savings Goals). Get to sharing with your accountability partner(s) and share them with me as well.

You can find me here:

Twitter / Instagram: @thebudgetnista
Facebook: The Budgetnista
Forum: www.livericherchallenge.com (Go to the website and request to join the private LIVE RICHER forum.)

My savings goals are...

_____

_____

_____

_____

_____

_____

_____

Live Richer Challenge: Savings Edition
Day 2: The First Law of Gold

Week 1: Savings Mindset

Today's Easy Financial Task: Read "The First Law of Gold" in the *Richest Man of Babylon.*

How to rock this task:
- Find *The Richest Man in Babylon (book)*
- Read "The First Law of Gold".
- Discuss the takeaway from this "law" with me and your accountability partners.
- Share how you'll use this "law" to build wealth.

Kudos, you've made it to Day 2!

Today we're taking the next step to improve your Savings Mindset.

To ditch a poverty mindset, it's essential to immerse yourself in inspirational and positive financial information, and that's exactly what you're going to do today. I want you to read "The First Law of Gold" from one of my favorite financial books, *The Richest Man in Babylon.*

Each principle in this book by George Clason will completely change the way you view saving forever. The book is a quick read that will have you living a richer life before you know it!

Don't worry. You're not going to read the whole book today. I just want you to focus on, "The First Law of Gold". It's one paragraph; it'll take you less than a minute. Afterwards, reflect on "The First Law of Gold" and think about how you'll apply it to your life. Then share how you will use it to foster a saving mindset with your accountability partners.

You can get a free .PDF copy of the book online by doing a quick search for it in a search engine. After you're finished reading, don't forget to share what you've learned today with me and your accountability partners.

Twitter / Instagram: @thebudgetnista
Facebook: The Budgetnista
Forum: www.livericherchallenge.com (go to the website and request to join the LIVE RICHER forum.)

I'll use the "The First Law of Gold" to...

_____

_____

_____

_____

_____

_____

_____

_____

_____

_____

_____

_____

Live Richer Challenge: Savings Edition
Day 3: The Money Bucket for Savings

Week 1: Savings Mindset

Today's Easy Financial Task: Open a Money Bucket to stockpile your savings.

How to rock this task:
- Visit the website www.MagnifyMoney.com to find a free Savings/Money Market Account (MMA) that has no fees.
- Select the free account that offers the highest interest rate.
- Apply to the account.

Today we're opening up a Money Bucket Account. What's a Money Bucket?

After it rains, the water disappears. Why? Because the ground soaks it up. You're just like the ground. When it rains money on payday, you too soak up the water a.k.a. your paycheck. You need to save some of that "rain" (income) with a bucket.

The perfect place for a Money Bucket is an online-only Savings Account or Money Market Account (MMA). So today I want you to sign up for one. Opening an account can take anywhere from a few minutes to a few days. Make sure you apply for your Money Bucket today because you'll need it for next week's tasks.

Why choose an account at an online-only bank?
- It's FREE. Yay! (At least it should be. Choose a free, no-fee Savings Account from www.MagnifyMoney.com)
- There's no minimum or maximum amount of money you can transfer into your Money Bucket. You can transfer $5 just as easily as $500.
- It takes 2-5 business days to transfer money from the online-only account (your Money Bucket) back to your regular bank account at your physical bank. This makes accessing your money inconvenient and inconvenient money gets saved. (Don't open a checking account at the

same online-only bank where you have your Money Bucket. You'll be able to use a debit card to spend your savings or make transfers quickly. Not a good idea.)

The purpose of this task is to show you how easy it can be to start saving. When you open your first Money Bucket, all you have to do is put money in it once per week—even if it's only a small amount. During next week's tasks, I'll also show you ways to cut expenses so you can save even more money!

One more thing: don't just choose any online account. Use this checklist to help you select the right account for your Money Bucket at www.MagnifyMoney.com.

Look for a Money Bucket/Online Savings Account That:
- Is FDIC-insured. (This is essential. "FDIC-insured" means that the Federal Government insures your money in the bank up to $250,000.)
- Has no fees.
- Has no minimum balance requirement.
- Has the highest interest rate available.
- Bonus: Find out if opening an account requires a hard inquiry. A hard inquiry on your credit history can impact your credit score by a few points.

Know someone who needs help with saving? Share the wealth and pass along Day 3's Easy Financial Task. Then share your progress with your accountability partner and with me via our private online forum accessible at www.livericherchallenge.com.

Live Richer Challenge: Savings Edition
Day 4: Purposeful Spending

Week 1: Savings Mindset

Today's Easy Financial Task: Identify your needs, loves, likes, and wants.

How to rock this task:
• List your basic *needs* like food, shelter, or water.
• Choose two *loves* and write them down.
• Share your *loves* with your accountability partners.

Today, we're going to discuss the four questions you should ask yourself before spending your hard-earned money on anything.

Do I:
1) **Need it?**
2) **Love it?**
3) **Like it?**
4) **Want it?**

Let's talk about your *needs* first.

Needs are the very basics, like food, shelter, or clothing. A *need* is something you must have in order to **live.** You need shelter to protect your family and without food you can't survive.

Next, come up with two things you *love.*

Understanding what you love is **key.** Things we *like* and *want* tend to cost less money and take less patience to acquire. On the other hand, things we *love* tend to cost more and take more sacrifice to obtain.

Drawing a blank on what you *love?*

Consider this: If you had Oprah's bank account, what would you do? Choose two of the things you imagine yourself having or doing; they're the financial *loves* of your life.

In order to save more money, it's important that we make the switch to a purposeful and passionate financial life.

Needs = purpose

Loves = passion

Spending less money on likes or wants means you'll have more money for savings and passions that add abundance to your life. We'll talk about this more later in the Challenge. Keep in mind that you don't have to cut out every single one of your likes and wants. It's just important that you establish priorities.

After you've put some thought into each category, share your loves with me and your accountability partner.

Remember, I can be found here:
Twitter & Instagram: @TheBudgetnista
Facebook: The Budgetnista
LIVE RICHER Forum: www.li009richerchallenge.com

My *loves* are...

_____

_____

_____

_____

_____

_____

Live Richer Challenge: Savings Edition
Day 5: Make a Move

Week 1: Savings Mindset

Today's Easy Financial Task: Take action toward a goal.

How to rock this task:
- Choose one goal from Day 1 of the Live Richer Challenge: Savings Edition.
- Commit to doing something easy today that will bring you closer to accomplishing that goal.
- Share what you're going to do today with your accountability partners.

Guess what? Today is our first task that includes a video. Yay! Visit www.livericherchallenge.com (Day 5: Make a Move; under the book resource tab) and take a moment to watch how to make today's task work for you. Then share what you're doing to reach your goal with your accountability partners.

The purpose of this task is to take action, no matter how small. One of the biggest obstacles that holds us back from success is the inability to overcome mental roadblocks. These hurdles impede our action or progress.

Here's how to get started:
1) Identify the goal your action will affect.
2) Identify how close you are to accomplishing that goal.
3) Ask yourself, "Self, what is the best next step that I can take toward making that goal happen?"
4) Take that step.

Note: Make sure the step can be taken today. No step is too small. What you're working on is your action-taking habit, so don't get caught up on whether or not the step is big enough.

Example:
1) Goal: To save $600 in 6 months.
2) I already have $50 saved.
3) I have $50 saved in cash. I can open up a Money Bucket (an online-only Savings Account) and save it there instead.
4) I go to www.MagnifyMoney.com and I find and open my Money Bucket.

If you want to save like a pro, you must repeat positive behaviors over time. Why? Often we can't make huge changes to our habits quickly, but we can make smaller changes more consistently. Today, my friend, you'll take one small step to adjust your savings behavior. Then next week, you'll create a plan of action to take several more steps toward your goal by the end of this Challenge, so get ready!

Today I'm taking action! I will...

1) Identify goal. My goal is to _____

_____

2) How close am I to goal? _____

_____

3) I will take action toward my goal today by _____

_____

4) I did it! *insert happy-dance* _____

_____

Live Richer Challenge: Savings Edition
Day 6: Review, Reflect, Relax

Week 1: Savings Mindset

Today's Easy Financial Task: Review, Reflect, Relax

How to rock this task:
- *Review* this week's Live Richer Challenge: Savings Edition tasks.
- *Reflect* on the changes you've made and your new Savings Mindset.
- *Relax.* In two days we start Week 2: Implementation & Automation.

Round of applause!

You've completed the first week of the Live Richer Challenge: Savings Edition. Woo hoo!

Take this day to review, reflect, and relax.

Share what you've learned and how you feel about the process with me and with your accountability partners. Remember, you can reach out to me here:

Twitter & Instagram: @TheBudgetnista
Facebook: The Budgetnista
LIVE RICHER Forum: www.livericherchallenge.com (Go to the website and request to join the LIVE RICHER forum.)

Don't forget: It's great to be helped, but it's even greater to use what you've been given to help someone else. Share the wealth and pass the Live Richer Challenge: Savings Edition along to someone you know who is struggling to save money.

Live Richer Challenge: Savings Edition
Day 7: Weekly Inspiration

Week 1: Money Mindset

Today's Easy Financial Task: Today's our first Dream Catcher Hangout Video to Hangout Chat!

How to Rock this task:
- Watch the chat.
- Listen to words of encouragement.
- Complete Challenge tasks you missed.

Today's our first Dream Catcher Hangout video!

During the video, we'll discuss the tasks we've worked on this week. We'll also talk about the key takeaways and you'll hear how other Dream Catchers like yourself are working through the challenge.

After watching, use this day to catch up on any tasks that you missed throughout the week. (Make sure you've signed up for a Money Bucket account because you'll need it for future Challenge days.) Tomorrow we have a fresh new week full of different savings tasks!

Watch the Dream Catcher Hangout here: www.liaricherchallenge.com under the book resources tab (Day 7: Weekly Inspiration).

Week 1: Savings Mindset Recap Checklist

○ **Day 1:** Easy Financial Task: Choose your savings goals, write them down, and share them with someone.

○ **Day 2:** Easy Financial Task: Read "The First Law of Gold" in the Richest Man of Babylon.

○ **Day 3:** Easy Financial Task: Open a Money Bucket to stockpile your savings.

○ **Day 4:** Easy Financial Task: Identify your needs, loves, likes, and wants.

○ **Day 5:** Easy Financial Task: Take action towards a goal.

○ **Day 6:** Easy Financial Task: Review, Reflect, Relax.

○ **Day 7:** Easy Financial Task: Watch the Week 1 Dream Catcher Hangout Chat.

Week 1 Reflections

_____

_____

_____

_____

_____

_____

_____

WEEK 2: IMPLEMENTATION & AUTOMATION

THIS WEEK'S GOAL:

To create a strategy to accomplish your savings goals.

Live Richer Challenge: Savings Edition
Day 8: Essential Spending

Week 2: Implementation & Automation

Today's Easy Financial Task: Kick non-essential spending to the curb.

How to rock this task:
- Only buy things you **need** today. Cut out all non-necessities like coffee, tea or lunch. (Don't worry—you won't have to starve. Just bring lunch from home.)
- Write down each time you **want** to spend money.
- Add up how much you save.
- Put the money you save at the end of the day into your Money Bucket.
- Share how much you save with your accountability partners.

Welcome to Week 2!

You've made it through an entire week of the Savings Challenge. Give yourself a pat on the back. Get ready for a full week of activities that will help you gain control of your money.

Today, your mission is to calculate how much you spend daily on things that are non-essential. After completing this task, you'll see just how much money you can save when you stop making small non-essential purchases here and there. Trust me: if you want to see your savings account grow, you must get a handle on your spending.

Once you've calculated what you've saved by not spending money throughout the day, you're going to take this task one step further.

Remember the Money Bucket we created last week? Transfer the money that you save today into your Money Bucket, no matter how small. Then commit to having at least one "essential spending only" day per week and you'll begin to see your Money Bucket grow before your eyes. Ready, set, go!

I put $_____ in my Money Bucket today! I did NOT buy....

_____

_____

_____

_____

_____

_____

_____

_____

_____

I'm very excited to hear how much you were able to save today, so share your savings commitment with me and your accountability partners. Don't forget to check into the LIVE RICHER forum to get connected with other Dream Catchers working through this task. Remember, you can reach out to me here:

Twitter / Instagram: @thebudgetnista
Facebook: The Budgetnista
Forum: www.livericherchallenge.com (Go to the website and request to join the LIVE RICHER forum by clicking the word "Forum".)

Live Richer Challenge: Savings Edition
Day 9: The Budget

Week 2: Implementation & Automation

Today's Easy Financial Task: Create a budget using the first chapter of my book *The One Week Budget.*

How to rock this task:
- Grab Day 1 of *The One Week Budget* for free at www.livericherchallenge. com (Click the tab marked "Book Resources" and go to "Day 9: The Budget").
- Read the first chapter to learn how to create a Money List (a.k.a. budget).
- Fill out your Money List using the template provided.
- Write down how much you spend *monthly* on each expense on your Money List
- Add up your expenses and subtract the amount from your *monthly* take-home pay. This will show you if have any money left over to save. (If you're not saving at all, it's okay; you'll learn how to save more money tomorrow.)

Today we have another video! Woop woop!

This is the most *important* day of the Challenge. I repeat: TODAY is the most important day of the Live Richer Challenge: Savings Edition. How much money you save rests upon your ability to properly budget. It's so critical that I'm going to walk you through creating a basic budget step-by-step here and in a video. You can watch my video at www. livericherchallenge.com via the tab marked "Book Resources" under "Day 10: The Budget".

Get excited!

Creating your budget may feel overwhelming at first, but I'm here to guide you through the process. Before you watch the video, please read the three steps in Day 1 of my bestselling book ***The One Week Budget*** (it won't take you very long). If you don't have much time, here's a condensed version of the steps for you in case you want to get started now:

Step 1 Create a List of your Spending Habits: a Money List.

Create a Money List by writing down all of your expenses.

Step 2 Show me the money.

Write the monthly cost of each expense on your Money List. Put your Monthly Take Home Pay on the top of your Money List.

Step 3 Money in the Bank: Savings

Calculate your Savings by adding up your Monthly Spending and subtracting it from your Monthly Take Home Pay. Fill in the amounts for Monthly Spending, Beginning Savings and Total. For today, fill out the full sheet provided **except** for the Reduced Monthly Amount column. Leave that blank. We'll tackle that later on in the Challenge.

For today, your only job is to fill out these parts of your Money List, including the Name of Expense, Monthly Amount and Due Date sections. We'll tackle the rest later on in the Challenge. Remember to share the budgeting skills you've learned with me, your accountability partners, and the Dream Catchers in the LIVE RICHER Forum.

Here's a blank Money List Template you can use to complete today's task. (You can also download a free digital copy at www.livericherchallenge.com via the "Book Resources" tab under "Day 10: The Budget".)

My Money List

NAME OF EXPENSE	CURRENT MONTHLY AMOUNT	REDUCED MONTHLY AMOUNT	DUE DATE
MONTHLY TAKE HOME PAY			
MONTHLY SPENDING			
		subtract	
SAVINGS (take home pay - total spending)			
TOTAL			
SAVINGS (Take Home Pay - Total Spending)			

Live Richer Challenge: Savings Edition
Day 10: Find Money

Week 2: Implementation & Automation

Easy Financial Task 11: Determine ways to save on your monthly expenses.

How to Rock This Task:
- Take out your Money List (budget) from yesterday's task.
- Go through each line item on your Money List to find areas where you can save money.
- Call your service providers and ask for a discount.
- Update each line item of your Money List with your savings in the Reduced Monthly Amount column.

Yesterday, you created a Money List (budget). Round of applause! You're killing it!

Today, it's time to find opportunities for savings. Take out your Money List and go through each expense to see if you can reduce the amount of money you spend for things like groceries, personal care, entertainment, transportation, etc. No amount is too small. Every bit you save will help you complete the savings tasks you wrote down on "Day 1: Savings Goals".

Next, call the service providers on your list, like your car insurance and cable providers to ask for a discount. Yup, I'm serious! Call them up and negotiate a discount.

We did this during the first Live Richer Challenge and tons of Dream Catchers (those of us doing the Live Richer Challenge) were able to successfully lower their bills. Do this task every year to ensure you're always getting the best deal from your service providers. You never want to miss out on opportunities to save money.

Don't think it can work? Here are a few success story from the first Live Richer Challenge:

Mrs. Sparks

What a blessing! I called my cell phone, cable and internet, and home security providers and was able to get a total reduction of about $70 a month! It's not a lot, but it's something! Money I can save and use towards my "LOVE" items in six months!

KiraATL

I've was able to save $30 on my cell phone bill. Yeah! Additionally, I received $21 off my auto insurance six month premium. I was an avid couponer at one time; I will have to bring that system back regularly. I saved a lot of money when I couponed previously. I just ran out of toothpaste after 2 years. LOL!

40 and Finding Fitness

I am enjoying this Challenge so far. I had to do a mental check and truly look at my expenses. I realized that my phone package had bells and whistles that I didn't need so I lowered my bill by about $80 by simply looking at how I was using my data plan. I also cancelled my cable since all the shows I watch are on regular TV. I simply purchased a $10 antenna and, voila, all the channels I need to see are clear. No more cable rip-off schemes.

Do you feel nervous about making the call? No worries—here's a script to help you.

The Script:

"Hello, my name is _____ and I've been a loyal customer for _____ years. I was reviewing my bill from your agency and due to financial constraints, I'm not able to continue paying this amount. I want to remain a customer; is there something you can do to help me?"

Do's and Don'ts of Asking For a Discount

- **Be pleasant.** The person on the phone has way more power than you think. They can pull strings behind the scenes, but they'll only do it if you treat them well. So be nice. Ask how their day is going; say thank you and that you appreciate their help.

- **Be persistent.** Sure, the first person you talk to may say no. That doesn't mean the next person will. Try, try, try again.

- **Do some research.** Find out competitor rates and use them to politely negotiate. Don't be afraid to drop their competitor's name while negotiating, too.

- **Ask for the Retention Department.** If you keep hearing no, ask for this department as a final resort. They'll be the most willing to make a deal as a last ditch effort to keep your business.

- **Be prepared to leave.** If your providers aren't willing to work with you and you really want to put more money into savings, you may have to cancel it. I cancelled my cable several years ago after getting too many no's. Now I use that money to travel instead. Best decision ever.

When you find savings, add it to yesterday's Money List in the Reduced Monthly Amount column. If you can't make any cuts to a line item, don't worry. Move on to the next one. I can't wait to hearing your savings success stories. Share them with me and your accountability partners! Remember, you can find me here:

Twitter / Instagram: @thebudgetnista
Facebook: The Budgetnista
Forum: www.liversicherchallenge.com (Go to the website and request to join the LIVE RICHER forum, by clicking the word "Forum".)

Live Richer Challenge: Savings Edition
Day 11: Restructure Your Debt

Week 2: Implementation & Automation

Today's Easy Financial Task: Lower the amount you pay in interest on your debt by restructuring it.

How to rock this task:
- Make a list of your debt. Include your creditor's name, amount owed, interest rate and minimum monthly payment.
- Lower how much you pay each month for debt using three different strategies.

Welcome back! Yesterday's task was great practice for what you're going to do today: negotiate. Did you know that you can pay less each month toward your debt and still pay it down faster? Yup! I'm going to show you three ways you can begin to do so today.

But first...

Use the My Debt List template to help you create a visual picture of the debt you owe. You'll find it at the end of today's task. (You can also download a free digital copy at www.liChallenge.com via the "Book Resources" tab under "Day 11: Restructure Your Debt".)

After you fill out the My Debt List sheet, it's time to tackle how to restructure your debt so you can pay less each month. Here are three things you can do today to help you do just that:

1) Call your credit card company(ies) and negotiate for lower rates. The higher your credit score, the more likely they are to work with you. Use the same script I gave you yesterday in "Day 10: Find Money" to help you negotiate.

2) Transfer the balance of your higher interest rate credit card(s) onto a lower interest rate card(s).

Wondering how to do a balance transfer? Here's how:

Go to www.magnifymoney.com and search for a balance transfer card. Look for a card that offers a 0% interest rate for at least six months and the lowest transfer fee available. Take note that when doing a balance transfer, credit card companies will often charge you a fee of about 3% of the total balance you're transferring.

FYI: Sometimes credit card companies run a special where you can transfer your balance without a fee. That's the type of deal you're looking for on www.magnifymoney.com.

Once you locate a card you're interested in, call the company and ask:

- How long will the 0% introductory rate last?

- What will my rate be after the introductory rate expires?

- What happens if I have **not** paid off my balance after my introductory rate expires? Will I be charged the new rate on the *full* balance or on the balance I have yet to pay off? This is SUPER important to know.

- How much is the transfer fee?

- What happens if I'm late with a payment?

- How much am I likely to be approved for? You don't want to have $8,000 in credit card debt and only be approved for $2,500. It's happened to me because I forgot to ask this question.

- Is there any fine print that I should know about?

Note: If your credit isn't decent, you may not qualify for a balance transfer card. No worries—you have another option which I explain in #3.

3) Look into taking out a low-interest rate loan and paying off those high-interest rate cards and student loans. This is another way to restructure your debt and save on interest.

Let's start with getting a loan for your high-interest credit cards, then I'll explain how to do the same for your student loans.

How to use a loan to restructure your credit card debt and save:
- Use your My Debt List to:

    - Add up how much credit card debt you have.

    - Calculate your average interest rate by adding up your all of your credit cards' rates and dividing that number by the amount of cards you have. You'll need to know your average interest rate so you can compare and identify a good deal when you try and refinance your debt.

- Determine your credit score. Use site like www.CreditKarma.com to get an estimate of your credit score for free.

    - Head to www.magnifymoney.com and search under "Personal Loans". You're looking for:

    - A company that Magnify Money has given an B+ or better.

    - A company that will give you a rate without a credit inquiry. Whenever you apply for credit, you generate a hard inquiry on your credit report. Hard inquires bring down your score and stay on your credit report for two years. You don't want that, so choose a company that does not generate an inquiry.

    - A company that offers a fixed term, fixed interest rate and no prepayment penalties.

    - A company that does not charge upfront fees.

Still not sure what company to choose? Don't worry. I have a company that I personally recommend and love. They've even given me a special Dream Catchers deal to share specifically with my readers.

Head to www.livericherchallenge.com under the "Book Resources" tab to "Day 11: Restructure Your Debt", to get my personal loan company suggestion.

How to restructure your student loan debt and save:
- Log onto your student loan company's website.

    - Determine if your student loan debt is a private student loan or a federal loan.

    - Note: This is SUPER important. If your loans are federal loans, do not—I repeat, DO NOT—refinance them with a private company. Here's why: the federal government offers a certain level of protection to federal student loan borrowers.

- Examples:

    - It takes 9 months of missed payments to default on a federal loan. It takes one missed payment to default on a private loan. A student loan default will dramatically bring down your credit score. Think, bankruptcy and foreclosure. Yup! It's that serious.

    - If you're become disabled, unemployed or are experiencing financial hardship, you can apply for forbearance or deferment of your federal loans. Most private loans do not have this option.

    - If you work in a specific (i.e. teacher, nonprofit etc), you can apply for loan forgiveness if you have federal loans. Private loans do not have this option.

- If you're unsure if you have federal or private student loans, call your loan provider and ask. If you have federal loans and are having trouble paying, ask to apply for an income based repayment program and any other program that you might be eligible for. Just make sure to keep your federal loans, federal.

- If you have private loans, follow these steps:

    - Add up how much student loan debt you have.

    - Calculate your average interest rate by adding up your all of your private student loan rates and dividing that number by the amount of loans you have. You'll need to know your average interest rate so you can compare and identify a good deal when you try and refinance your loan.

- Determine your credit score. Use site like www.CreditKarma.com to get an estimate of your credit score for free.

Head to www.magnifymoney.com and search under "Student Loan Refinance". You're looking for:

- A company that Magnify Money has given an B+ or better.

- A company that has no origination fee. An origination fee is an up-front fee charged by a lender for processing a new loan application, used as compensation for putting the loan in place. It's usually a percentage of the loan.

- A company that has no max. It offers graduates the ability to refinance qualified education loans.

Again, still not sure what company to choose? Head to www.livericherchallenge.com under the "Book Resources" tab to "Day 11: Restructure Your Debt", to find out more about the special Dream Catcher deal offered by my recommended, private student loan refinancing company.

Whew! I know, I know. Today is going to be a busy day. Don't let all of the steps discourage you from taking action today. It's really just three things:

1) Call and negotiate a lower interest rate on your existing credit cards.

2) Consider transferring your current credit card balance to a lower interest rate balance transfer card. You'll need good credit.

3) Consider refinancing your debt, credit card debt and private student loans with a refinancing company that offers lower interest rates.

4) Use my recommendations at www.livericherchallenge.com under the "Book Resources" tab under "Day 11: Restructure Your Debt" to help you.

That's it!

I know these work. I myself have done #1 and #2 with great success. I've also coached a number of clients, friends and family on #3. As a result, many of them have saved thousands of dollars a year. Yes, that much!

So what are you waiting for? Your dreams aren't going to fund themselves. They need your help. Let's knock today's task out of the park.

I'm really excited to hear how much you were able to save as a result of today's task. Check in with your accountability partner and report back to your fellow Dream Catchers in our forum too.

Remember, you can reach out to me here:
Twitter / Instagram: @thebudgetnista
Facebook: The Budgetnista
Forum: www.livericherchallenge.com (go to the website and request to join the LIVE RICHER forum, by clicking the word forum.)
Forum: www.livericherchallenge.com

My Debt List
(NOTE: List debt lowest to highest)

NAME OF DEBT	TOTAL AMT. OWED	MIN. MONTHLY PMT.	INTEREST RATE	DUE DATE	STATUS

Live Richer Challenge: Savings Edition
Day 12: Automate Your Savings

Week 2: Implementation & Automation

Today's Easy Financial Task: Automate the savings that goes into your Money Bucket.

How to rock this task:
- Automate your savings from Day 10's "Find Money" task into your Money Bucket from Day 3.

So far this week, you've had a no-spend day, created a budget, found savings by negotiating with your service providers, and restructured your debt. Today we're talking automation.

Automation = The New Discipline

You're 100% more likely to stick to your savings goals when money is automatically transferred into your savings account. Let's face it: humans can be pretty unreliable. Automated transfers however are *completely* reliable.

Your task today is to set up automatic transfers to your Money Bucket. Where will the money come from? Glad you asked!

Did you call your service providers and save money during Day 10's task, "Find Money"? If yes, AWESOME! You just need to save the money you'll now have from reducing your bills.

Here's how:
1) List the due dates of the recurring payments of each service provider who agreed to lower your bill on your Money List.

2) Instead of paying the full amount to your providers, transfer the amount that you're saving to your Money Bucket. Make the two payments on the same day you normally pay the service provider.

3) Automate both payments, part of it to the service provider and part of it to your Money Bucket.

For example: Your phone bill was $300/month and you negotiated it down to $200/month, a savings of $100. Instead of spending the discount on new shoes, you decide to save it. Your cable bill is due on the 10th of every month. You pay $300/month on the 10th: $200 goes to cable and $100 goes to your Money Bucket with both payments automated.

You can also find other savings to put into your Money Bucket. Try committing to an "essential spending only" day one day each the week. Have you found savings on your other monthly expenses like groceries, personal care, or transportation? Add up how much you can comfortably save monthly and set up another automatic transfer to your Money Bucket.

Still need help? I've found and personally use an awesome **free** app that will analyze your income and spending and find small amounts of money it can safely set aside for you. Yup! You can get a link to this app at www.livericherchallenge.com under the "Book Resources" tab in "Day 12: Automate Your Savings".

No more excuses, my friend.

You have all the tools you need to reduce your spending in order to save money automatically. Next week, we're going to discuss ways to make more money for your savings goals and passions. Get excited!

Remember to support your accountability partners. This is a team effort! Are they keeping up with the Challenge? Have they automated their savings? Hold them accountable!

Live Richer Challenge: Savings Edition
Day 13: Review, Reflect, Relax

Week 2: Implementation & Automation

Today's Easy Financial Task: Review, Reflect, Relax

How to rock this task:
- *Review* this week's Live Richer Challenge: Savings Edition tasks.
- *Reflect* on the changes you've made to implement and automate your savings.
- *Relax.* In two days we start Week 3: Increase Your Abundance.

Happy Dance

You've completed the second week of the Live Richer Challenge: Savings Edition. You're truly a super star! Take this day to review, reflect, and relax. Share what you've learned and how you feel about the process with me and with your accountability partners. Remember, you can reach out to me here:

Twitter / Instagram: @thebudgetnista
Facebook: The Budgetnista
Forum: www.livericherchallenge.com
(Go to the website and request to join the LIVE RICHER forum.)

> Don't forget: it's great to be helped, but it's even greater to use what you've been given to help someone else. Share the wealth and pass the Live Richer Challenge: Savings Edition along to someone you know who is struggling to master saving.

Live Richer Challenge: Savings Edition
Day 14: Weekly Inspiration Check

Week 2: Implementation & Automation

Today's Easy Financial Task 14: Watch the Week 2 Dream Catcher Hangout Chat.

How to rock this task:
- Watch the chat.
- Listen to words of encouragement.
- Complete any Challenge tasks you missed.

Today's our second Dream Catcher Hangout video!

During the video, we'll discuss the tasks we've worked on this week. We'll also talk about the key takeaways and you'll hear how other Dream Catchers, like yourself, are working through the Challenge.

You should also use this day to catch up on any tasks that you missed during the week. Tomorrow we have a fresh new week full of different tasks to help you save and make money!

Watch the Dream Catcher Hangout here: www.livericherchallenge.com under "Day 14: Weekly Inspiration".

Week 2: Implementation & Automation Checklist

○ **Day 8:** Easy Financial Task: Kick non-essential spending to the curb.

○ **Day 9:** Easy Financial Task: Create a budget using the first chapter of my book, *The One Week Budget.*

○ **Day 10:** Easy Financial Task: Locate ways to save on your monthly expenses.

○ **Day 11:** Easy FInancial Task: Restructure your debt for savings.

○ **Day 12:** Easy Financial Task: Automate the savings that goes into your Money Bucket.

○ **Day 13:** Easy Financial Task: Review, Reflect, Relax.

○ **Day 14:** Easy Financial Task: Watch the Week 2 Dream Catcher Hangout chat.

Week 2 Reflections

_____

_____

_____

_____

_____

_____

_____

WEEK 3: INCREASE YOUR ABUNDANCE

THIS WEEK'S GOAL:

To attract abundance and identify ways to increase your earnings.

Live Richer Challenge: Savings Edition
Day 15: Activate Abundance

Week 3: Increase Your Abundance

Today's Easy Financial Task: Learn what abundance means and how to activate it in your life.

How to rock this task:
- Watch the video on activating abundance.
- Choose the abundance you want to add to your budget.
- Share your thoughts with me and your accountability partners.

Welcome to Week 3, my friend!

Today is Week 3's video day. Can you believe we're nearing the end of our Challenge? Me neither! Still, we have a lot left to do, so roll up your sleeves.

During the first two weeks of our Live Richer Challenge: Savings Edition, we focused on ways to cut expenses in order to boost your savings. This week we're going to discuss how to *make more money* so you can add your *loves* to your budget. Remember your *loves* from Week 1's "Day 4: Purposeful Spending"? Pull them back out.

Money is *one* of the tools that can help you to live a more abundant life. With money you can give more, experience more and create more opportunities. When you plan, budget and save, you can do the things that really matter to you, like traveling, starting a business, volunteering or funding a new hobby.

Visit www.livericherchallenge.com and go to the "Book Resources" tab to "Day 15: Activate Abundance" and take a moment to watch how to make today's task work for you.

Here are the key takeaways from the video.

How to Attract Abundance:

1) Begin with Gratefulness: Being grateful signifies that you acknowledge what you *do* have vs. what you don't have. Remember; what you water blooms. This means if you focus on what you don't have, you create an atmosphere of lack. If you focus on what you do have, you create an atmosphere of abundance. The choice is yours.

2) Your Perspective: Decide today that **you** are worthy of what you seek. You are! Also, know that just because things are hard, doesn't mean that they're not working. Sometimes life calls for hard times. You learn the most valuable lessons during those times. Use those lessons to maximize the good and great times. Shift your perspective. Both the good and "bad" times are necessary for growth and abundance.

3) Your Generosity: Giving activates abundance. When you give honestly and genuinely, you're projecting that you have extra, that you have more than enough. When you give from an honest, genuine place you create an opportunity to receive. Two things to keep in mind when you give:

   a) Give without expectation. Giving to receive is not true giving.
   b) You reap *what* you sow, but not always *where* you sow. Abundance can come from a totally different source than the one you gave to.

Now that you've watched the video, it's time to write down the abundance you want to add to your budget. Then share it with me, your accountability partner(s) and the Dream Catchers in the LIVE RICHER Forum.

Oh and one more thing: how are you progressing towards the goals you identified on Week 1's "Day 1: Savings Goals"? Are you on track to meet your savings goals in the timeframe you've chosen? Share your progress with me!

Twitter / Instagram: @thebudgetnista
Facebook: The Budgetnista
Forum: www.livericherchallenge.com
(Go to the website and request to join the LIVE RICHER forum.)

Live Richer Challenge: Savings Edition
Day 16: Add Abundance to Your Budget

Week 3: Increase Your Abundance

Today's Easy Financial Task: Calculate the total cost of your loves and add it to your Money List.

How to rock this task:
- Fill out your abundance worksheet with your loves from Day 4.
- Take out your Money List (aka budget) from Day 10.
- Add abundance to your Money List.
- Do the math to see how much extra money you need for abundance.

Another day, another task. Let's get to it!

Yesterday, you decided what abundance looks like in your life. The purpose of today's task is to see how much extra money you need to earn per month to make abundance happen.

Don't hold back; I want you to add everything you're passionate about. You may not have the funds right now to pay for it all, but it's important to pre-plan for the life you want so you can take the steps necessary to attain it.

To help you with today's task, I've created an Abundance Worksheet. You can get a copy of it at www.livericherchallenge.com under "Day 16: Add Abundance to Your Budget". Use the worksheet to estimate how much your abundance costs each month. Then put the total from your abundance worksheet on the abundance line of your Money List.

Here's an example. If I want to get my hair done for $200 and piano lessons for $150 per month, I write it all down on my Abundance Worksheet. The total is $350. Then I write $350 on the abundance line of my Money List.

Make sense?

After you've added abundance to your budget, do the math to see how much more money you need to make each month to cover abundance. Do this by taking a look at your newly designated savings. Can a portion of that money be set aside to fund your abundance? If so, how much more do you need to make to cover the rest? If you don't want to use some of your savings, that's okay; that just means you'll have to make the full about to fund your abundance desires.

Share how much more you need to make per month to pay for abundance with your accountability partner(s).

I will need to make $_____ per month to activate abundance.

The abundance I want to add to my budget:

_____

_____

_____

_____

_____

_____

_____

_____

_____

_____

_____

_____

_____

Live Richer Challenge: Savings Edition
Day 17: Make Mo' Money

Week 3: Increase Your Abundance

Today's Easy Financial Task: Think of ways you can make extra income to pay for your loves (abundance).

How to rock this task:
- Brainstorm ways to use your skills, talents, and experience to make more money each month.
- Share how you plan to make extra income with me and your partner(s).

Cha-Ching!

Yesterday when you added abundance to your budget, you may have found you don't quite make enough money each month to cover it. No worries! I'm going to share a few tips and resources to help you make extra income outside of your job (if you have one). I highly recommend that you have have multiple sources of income (i.e. babysitting or tutoring). It can help you pay for your abundance **AND** help you to reach your savings goals much faster.

Ready to make mo' money? Fabulous! Let's get down to business.

First, I have three quick pointers you should keep in mind when deciding what you should do for extra income:

1. **Use Your Degree.** If you have the education, put it to use. You can charge more money for a service when you're an expert in a field. Think about how you can shape your education into an extra source of income.

2. **Do What You Do For a Living.** You can hit the ground running with your side hustle if you have work experience in the industry. There's no learning curve and you have a resume that proves you know what you're doing.

3. **Activate Your Passion.** Start charging for things you already do for free. You already have an established clientele who like your work and you can use them to spread the word.

4. **Negotiate a Raise.** Start to collect all of the amazing value you bring to your job. Put it together in a file. Make sure you monetize your value. Example: The decision you made to do _____ is saving the company $10,000/year.

For other ways to make side income, www.ThePennyHoarder.com has an excellent resource called "32 Legitimate Ways to Make Money at Home". Here are a few favorites from the list:

• **Focus Groups**—Want to get paid for your opinion? The Penny Hoarder suggests ProOpinion to find online focus groups. You can also look to CraigsList or FocusGroup to get paid for participating in research studies.

• **Take Online Surveys**—Take surveys in your down time while watching TV or commuting on public transit and get paid for it. The Penny Hoard recommends Ipsos Panel, SendEarnings, MySurvey and Springboard Panel.

• **Make Money as a Transcriptionist**—Transcriptionists can make up to $25 per hour listening to audio and typing out what's said. This job could be right up your alley if you're a fast and accurate typer. Learn how to get started in the field on The Penny Hoarder post "Earn $25 an Hour as a Transcript".

• **Rent or Sell Clothes Online**—Do you have a full closet of clothes you don't wear? Sell or rent them for extra money. Head over to the sites Tradesy, Loanables and RentNotBuy to cash in on your unused clothes.

Do you have any more ideas to add to this list? Share with your accountability partner and in the Dream Catcher Forum. Your ideas may inspire another!

Be Careful of Scams

Keep your eyes peeled for jobs that appear suspicious, especially on Craigslist. You should never have to pay money to make money and get-rich-quick schemes don't exist. If a job sounds like a scam, it probably is.

Lastly, make sure your side hustle is worth your time and resources. If you drive an hour and spend $20 on parking just to make $25, you're breaking even. That isn't the type of hustle that will help you save much money or pay for abundance in your budget.

Now, it's time to get your abundance on.

My side hustle ideas are...

_____

_____

_____

_____

_____

_____

_____

_____

_____

_____

_____

_____

_____

_____

Live Richer Challenge: Savings Edition
Day 18: Your Abundance Plan

Week 2: Increase Your Abundance

Today's Easy Financial Task: Figure out how many hours you need to work to pay for your loves (abundance).

How to Rock This Task:
- Keeping in mind the amount of money you need for your loves, calculate the number of hours and rate at which you need to work each week to reach this goal.

You've made it to Day 18!

Are you excited to earn more income on the side? I'm excited for you. Today we're going to take yesterday's task one step further. You're going to figure out exactly how many hours you need to work to pay for your loves.

Always keep in mind, the reason you seek to earn more money isn't to work yourself to death. I don't believe in over-sacrifice. You should work to make exactly how much you need to meet your savings goals and live a more abundant life. No more.

Here's how to find out how much work that'll take:

Say I need to make an extra $350 per month for my loves. Since there are 4 weeks in a month, I need to make about $88 per week (or $350 divided by 4). I decide to babysit for $15 per hour. If I do, I need to make sure I get in about 6 hours of babysitting each week to reach my goal (or $88 divided by $15). Now it's your turn!

When you're finished doing the math, share how many hours you plan to work with your partner(s) and me.

Quick Reminder: How are you progressing toward your Savings Goals from Day 1? Keep me updated!

Twitter / Instagram: @thebudgetnista
Facebook: The Budgetnista
Forum: www.livericherchallenge.com
(Go to the website and request to join the LIVE RICHER forum.)

I need to work _____ of my side hustle per week

to make _____.

Notes:

_____

_____

_____

_____

_____

_____

_____

_____

_____

_____

_____

_____

_____

Live Richer Challenge: Savings Edition
Day 19: Your Abundance Action Plan

Week 3: Increase Your Abundance

Today's Easy Financial Task: Take a step forward on your path to making more money.

How to rock this task:
- Do an activity today to begin side hustling.
- Share what action you're taking with me and your accountability partner(s).

Congrats! We're almost at the end of our third week.

How are you feeling? How are you progressing with your savings goals from Day 1? There's still three more days left to take a concrete step to reach it! Keep pushing.

Today we're going to put your abundance plan in motion. You're going to do an activity that will help you start making extra money ASAP.

Growing up, one of my father's favorite sayings was "Many drops of water does a mighty river make." This means a series of small choices can add up to big results.

What small choices can you do today? Now?

Things You Can Do to Put Your Abundance in Action:
- Search Craigslist for studies in your area.
- Post a free ad on Craigslist or Angie's List about your product or service.
- Sign up for survey sites and take a few surveys.
- Mention your side hustle to everyone you see.
- Post photos on Facebook, Twitter or Instagram with information on your hustle.

- Send out a price list to let people know that you're now charging for your services.
- Sign up for studies on FocusGroup.com.
- Create a file of the value you've brought to your job, then ask your boss for an appointment to meet. Ask for that raise!

Extra income won't fall into your lap, but if you begin actively seeking opportunities to make money it'll start coming your way. In the long run, your small actions from today, tomorrow and into the future will make all the difference. So pick up the phone, send some emails, post your services on social media, and start networking! Do something today. At the very least tell me and your accountability partner your plans for making more.

What I'll do today to put my abundance plan in motion...

_____

_____

_____

_____

_____

_____

_____

_____

_____

_____

_____

Live Richer Challenge: Savings Edition
Day 20: Review, Reflect, Relax

Week 3: Increase Your Abundance

Today's Easy Financial Task: Review, Reflect, Relax

How to rock this task:
- *Review* this week's Live Richer Challenge: Savings Edition tasks.
- *Reflect* on the changes you've made to increase your abundance.
- *Relax.* Tomorrow is our last task, "Giving Back & LIVING RICHER".

You've completed the third week of the Live Richer Challenge: Savings Edition. You're truly a superstar! Take this day to review, reflect, and relax.

Share what you've learned and how you feel about the process with me and with your accountability partners. Remember, you can reach out to me here:

Twitter / Instagram: @thebudgetnista
Facebook: The Budgetnista
Forum: www.livericherchallenge.com
(Go to the website and request to join the LIVE RICHER forum.)

Don't forget: It's great to be helped, but it's even greater to use what you've been given to help someone else. Share the wealth and pass the Live Richer Challenge: Savings Edition along to someone you know who is struggling to master saving.

Live Richer Challenge: Savings Edition
Day 21: Weekly Inspiration Check

Week 3: Increase Your Abundance

Today's Easy Financial Task: Watch the Week 3 Dream Catcher Hangout.

How to rock this task:
- Watch the chat.
- Listen to words of encouragement.
- Complete any Challenge tasks you missed this week.

Today's our final Dream Catcher Hangout Chat!

During the video, we'll discuss the tasks we've worked on this week. We'll also talk about the key takeaways and you'll hear how other Dream Catchers, like yourself, are working through the Challenge.

You should also use this day to catch up on any tasks that you missed during the week. Tomorrow is our last Challenge day!

Watch the Dream Catcher Hangout here: www.livericherchallenge.com under the tab "Book Resources", "Day 21: Weekly Inspiration".

Week 3: Increase Your Abundance Checklist

○ **Day 15:** Easy Financial Task: Learn what abundance means and how to activate it in your life.

○ **Day 16:** Easy Financial Task: Calculate the total cost of your loves and add it to your Money List.

○ **Day 17:** Easy Financial Task: Think of ways you can make extra income to pay for your loves.

○ **Day 18:** Easy Financial Task: Calculate how many hours you need to work to make enough money for loves.

○ **Day 19:** Easy Financial Task: Take a step forward on your path to making more money.

○ **Day 20:** Easy Financial Task: Review, Reflect, Relax

○ **Day 21:** Easy Financial Task: Watch the Week 3 Week 3 Dream Catcher Hangout

Week 3 Reflections

_____

_____

_____

_____

_____

_____

DAY 22: LIVE RICHER

FINAL DAY'S GOAL:

To learn how to purposefully and passionately pursue an abundant life by using your finances as one of your tools.

Live Richer Challenge: Savings Edition
Day 22: Giving Back and Living Richer

Today's Easy Financial Task: Create a vision board of your ideal life and learn the importance of giving back.

How to rock this task:
- Make your vision board and post it.
- Report on your goal task progress from Day 1.
- Report on your savings goal progress from Day 1's task.

DrumrollTrumpets**Tambourines**

You've completed the Live Richer Challenge: Savings Edition. You rock! Now that you've completed the tasks, it's time to think about how savings and abundance affect your entire life.

We've discussed how money is one of the tools you can use to help you live a purposeful and passionate life. What does that life look like for you? What have you always dreamed of doing, seeing, attaining? Today's task is to envision what these things look, feel, taste, and smell like. One of the best ways to visualize your dreams is through a vision board. If you're not sure how to make one, head to www.liventicherchallenge.com under "Book Resources" under "Day 22: Giving Back and Living Richer". There I've provided a free resource for you called "**How to Make a Vision Board That Actually Works**".

Once you finish your vision board, post it somewhere you can see it daily: on your fridge, in your room, on your computer or phone. Look at it every-day to remind yourself of the reasons you save your money and hustle to earn extra income.

Goal Check In

In the beginning of the Challenge, weeks ago we wrote down our savings goals and committed to taking a number of steps toward our goal by the end of this Challenge. Have you taken any steps? If so, pat yourself on the back! Tell me and your accountability partners what you did so we can do a happy-dance in your honor.

If you didn't take any action, don't give up! Use what you've learned about saving and making more money during this Challenge to keep working towards your goal. Whenever you need help along the way, reach out to me and your Dream Catchers in the Dream Catcher Forum for support.

Although the Live Richer Challenge: Savings Edition has come to an end, your journey is just beginning and I'd love to be a part of it. Share your successes from the Challenge with me here:

Twitter / Instagram: @thebudgetnista
Facebook: The Budgetnista
Forum: www.livericherchallenge.com
(Go to the website and request to join the LIVE RICHER forum.)

One more thing...

Giving Back

I must stress this again: Giving activates abundance. It's great to be helped; it's greater to use what you've been given to help someone else. Share your time, energy, resources, and knowledge with those who have less than you. Commit to sharing your abundance with the world through small acts of kindness.

My small act was to create the Live Richer Challenge. As a result, thousands of Dream Catchers worldwide are now able to live better lives using the information I've shared. The overwhelming response I've gotten from people that completed my first Live Richer Challenge (this book is the second) was and still is overwhelming.

I'm blessed to be a blessing, and so are you.

Live richer,
Tiffany "The Budgetnista" Aliche

Live Richer Challenge Recap Checklist

○ **Week 1:** I completed my Savings Mindset tasks.

○ **Week 2:** I completed my Implementation & Automation tasks.

○ **Week 3:** I completed my Increase Your Abundance tasks.

○ **Day 22:** I'm actively working toward creating abundance, giving back and living a richer life.

Live Richer Challenge: Savings Edition Reflections:

_____

_____

_____

_____

_____

_____

_____

_____

_____

_____

_____

Acknowledgments:

First and foremost, I would like to give my most grateful thanks to God. He always blesses us. It is we who allow or do not allow our blessings to manifest.

I also want to thank Mommy, Daddy, and my sisters: Karen, Tracy, Carol, and Lisa. You are my cheerleaders, my best friends, my sounding board, and my inspiration. Anyone who knows the *Aliche Girls* knows how supportive we are of each other. Thank you.

To all my family, both here and abroad, thank you for your constant love and support. The strong foundation you've provided is the reason I've been able to reach such heights.

Taylor Medine and Ridhi Shetty, thank you so much for helping me transform and polish my words into a book I can be proud of.

Superman a.k.a. Jerrell, thank you for your unwavering support and love.

Thank you to my designer Hector Torres. I came to you at crunch time and you more than delivered.

Thank you, Sierra Kirby. I literally could not have launched the LIVE RICHER Challenge without you.

Special thanks to Linda Iferika, Dreena Whitfield, Jubril Agoro, all my family, friends, coworkers, and all of my well wishers.

Lastly, I especially want to thank you. Yes, you reading these words. You allowed me to help you LIVE RICHER. You gave me more than I ever gave you. I am forever grateful.

Tiffany "The Budgetnista" Aliche is an award-winning teacher of financial empowerment and is quickly becoming America's favorite financial educator. The Budgetnista specializes in the delivery of financial literacy and has served as the personal finance education expert for City National Bank.

Since 2008, The Budgetnista has been a brand ambassador and spokesperson for a number of organizations, delivering finan-cial education through seminars, workshops, curricula and trainings. In 2014, Tiffany founded the LIVE RICHER Challenge Movement, a virtual community of thousands from 50 states and 65+ countries.

Author of #1 Amazon bestseller *The One Week Budget* and *Live Richer Challenge*, Tiffany and her financial advice have been featured in *The New York Times, Reuters, US News and World Report, The TODAY Show,* PBS, Fox Business, MSNBC, CBS, *MoneyWatch, TIME, ESSENCE Magazine,* and *FORBES.* She regularly blogs about personal finance for *The Huffing-ton Post* and *U.S. News and World Report.*

Tiffany has also been has been a featured speaker at American Express, Princeton University, Wyndham Worldwide, Columbia University, MegaFest, The United Way, Prudential Financial Inc. and many more. The Budgetnista's client list includes Prudential, The NASDAQ OMX Group, JetBlue, Dress for Success and the NAACP.

You can learn more about Tiffany and The Budgetnista at www.thebudgetnista.com.

12974600R00042